CW00449221

1

Sociopath

Understand Antisocial Personality Disorder

Table of Contents

Introduction

A sociopath is a person who suffers from antisocial behavior. This term was not even existent a hundred years ago. In fact, the first version of antisocial personality disorder was published in 1952 but was not given a lot of importance because the complexity of this disorder is little understood. Today, it is estimated that 2.1% of the adult population in the United States suffer from antisocial disorder. This means that 1 in 47 suffers from antisocial personality disorder and this would translate to 5.7million of people in the United States alone. Aside from the United States, the antisocial personality disorder is also prevalent in countries like Canada, Mexico, Belize, Nicaragua, Denmark and Finland.

A person who suffers from this disorder is characterized with the incessant attitude of disregard towards other people. This means that they are not able to conform to what society defines as normal personality and they tend to become antisocial. Sociopaths also exhibit symptoms like physical aggression and the inability to sustain healthy relationship with others or hold down a steady job. Although there is a negative connotation associated with this condition, sociopaths can also have charm, confidence and wit but these attributed are often superficial as they are not really committed to feeling any deep emotions with others and might display good behavior to others as an aim to achieve their own personal agenda. Understanding antisocial personality disorder is a difficult task but this book aims to help you connect with a person who is suffering from this personality disorder.

Chapter 1: Understanding the Antisocial Personality Disorder

Sociopaths are people who suffer from antisocial personality disorder. People who suffer from this personality disorder often display the lack of empathy coupled with the display of abnormal moral conduct that deviates from the norms of society. People who suffer from this personality disorder are also often involved in crimes, drug and alcohol addiction because of their impulsive behavior. Sociopaths are also often unable to control their emotions and they easily resort to verbal abuse and aggression when faced with threats or with situations that are unappealing to them.

Causes of Antisocial Personality Disorder

Personality disorders are often commonly caused by the combination of both biological and environmental factors. Below is a discussion of the causes of antisocial personality disorder.

Biological Factors

One of the causes of personality disorder is biological factors. Many medical experts believe a person born with personality disorder often have different brain wirings that prevents them from learning from their mistakes or responding correctly to stress like fear and anger. Below are biological triggers why antisocial personality disorder develops.

- **Hormones and neurotransmitters:** The release of hormones can change patterns of development. For instance, the release of testosterone can lead to the aggressiveness of a person. Low levels of cortisol can also trigger impulsive behavior. On the other hand, several studies suggest that people who have lower levels of serotonin are also likely to suffer from personality disorders.

- **Limbic neural mal-development:** The limbic system is a set of brain structures located on the sides of the thalamus. It supports a wide array of function such as the emotion, motivation, behavior, long-term memory and adrenaline flow. This means that the emotional aspect of the brain is housed in this system. However, scientists have found out that people who suffer from maldevelopment of the limbic system are unable to process their emotions correctly which can lead to personality disorders.

- **Head injuries:** Many researches have linked head injuries to antisocial behavior. Scientists have associated traumatic brain injury that leads to damage of the prefrontal cortex to also cause antisocial personality disorder. A damaged prefrontal cortex leads to the inability to make socially and morally acceptable decisions and also leads to aggression. On the other hand, damage to the amygdale can also lead to aggressive behavior and loss of empathy.

Environmental Factors

On the other hand, the most common reason why people become sociopaths is more likely to be caused with environmental factors. Below is an in-depth discussion on the different environmental factors that can cause the antisocial personality disorders.

- **Experiences:** Experiences play a very important role to the development of antisocial personality disorder. The environmental causes of this personality disorder include any forms of deprivation, abandonment, sexual abuse and emotional abuse.

- **Examples:** Children who grew up with parents who also display antisocial behavior are also more likely to develop this personality disorder.

How to Recognize a Sociopath

While sociopath is a personality disorder associated with aggression, detecting sociopaths in a room full of people can be very difficult. In fact, even sociopaths themselves are not aware that they are already suffering from this condition thus they are able to avoid medical help. Moreover, sociopaths are really good in both deception and manipulation. It is therefore important that you proceed with caution if you think you are dealing with a sociopath. Also, it is crucial that you also know how to recognize one. Below are the warning signs that you are dealing with a sociopath.

- Inconsistency with what a person says or does.
- Lies repetitively for personal profit.
- Constantly makes excuses when caught in a lie.
- Inability to feel shame after being caught in an embarrassing situation.
- Ability to sense vulnerabilities in others and using those [vulnerabilities] for personal gain or for manipulating others.
- Inability to have empathy behind the rules and law.
- Repeatedly doing acts that can serve as bases for arrest.
- Disregard for safety for others or for oneself.
- Shows cruelty to animals.
- Readiness to blame others for their mistakes.
- Inability to feel any guilt or to learn from their experiences.
- Low tolerance to frustration and low threshold for the discharge of their aggression.

It is important to learn about the signs of this personality disorder. By doing so, you will be able to learn how to deal with them so that you will have a harmonious relationship with a person who is suffering from antisocial personality disorder.

Types of Sociopaths

It is important to learn how to differentiate between psychopathy and sociopathy. Although both are personality disorders that people often interchange with one another, people who suffer from the former are often suspicious or paranoid that is translated to their aggressive behavior. Moreover, psychopaths are capable of having normal relationship as well as holding successful careers. They also place a lot of emphasis on planning especially if they plan to commit a crime. Sociopaths, on the other hand, are incapable of having deep relationship with other people and are often disorganized as well as erratic. Although different, there is a thin line that separates the two thus this section will discuss the different types of antisocial personality disorder or sociopathy to understand that not all sociopaths display the same behavioral symptoms.

- **Entitled Sociopath:** This term involves the state of entitlement wherein a person who is suffering from this personality disorder has no ideals and does not feel shame in their actions. They also feel very satisfied in what they do – whether good or bad. Entitles sociopaths enjoy making fun of people in authority.

- **Amoral Sociopath:** An amoral sociopath commits deeds without any sense of remorse, guilt or awareness of moral strictures. They also have weak perception to pain thus these kinds of sociopaths tend to enjoy torturing animals or watch animals kill each other.

- **Common Sociopath:** Also termed as sub-cultural delinquents, common sociopaths have weak conscience as well as future perspective. However, they are still able to have relationships with other people albeit difficult. Most children who has one parent who is a common sociopath also grow up as one because either one of the parents or both provide a strong example to their kids.

- **Alienated Sociopath:** Alienated sociopaths are individuals who haven't developed the ability to affiliate with other people. An alienated sociopath has two sub-cultures and below is the discussion of the two types of alienated sociopaths:

  - ***Disaffiliated type:*** The disaffiliated sociopath is often a result of growing up in the absence of a nurturing parent. Children who grow up without learning the ability to love find it hard to reciprocate other people's emotions or understand others as well.

- ○ **Disempathic types:** This type of sociopath is capable of having emotional investment with people within his or her *circle of empathy*. This can mean that he is capable of loving his parents, friends and even his dog but reacts to most people only as objects.

- ○ **Hostile types:** Sociopaths react differently to external stimuli and hostile sociopaths are people who have aggressive and destructive attitude towards the members of the community.

- ○ **Cheated types:** Freud has mention about individuals who feels disadvantages by their physical disabilities, class origin, minority status or situation and thinks that they are always being cheated on because of their incapacities. Most sociopaths who are this type often feel that the world is out to get them and they tend to justify their reactions based on this assumption.

- **Theodore Million's Sociopath Subtypes:** Theodore Million was a celebrated American psychologist who worked on personality disorders. He developed five subtypes of sociopaths discussed below:

  - *Nomadic:* A person who is under this subtype often feels doomed and jinx. Because of their fears, they have the tendency to adapt a nomadic life by wandering from one place to the other as well as dropping out from work or school.

  - *Malevolent:* A malevolent sociopath is belligerent, brutal and resentful to people around him. They always anticipate betrayal from other people and desire revenge and punishment to people whom they think have wronged them.

o **Covetous:** A covetous sociopath feels deprived and denied of many things thus they discontentedly yearn for many things. They are envious, greedy and take a lot of pleasure in amassing things.

o **Risk-taking:** Risk taking types are dauntless and bold thus they tend to do a lot of reckless things without thinking about the welfare of people around them.

o **Reputation defending:** This type of sociopath always builds an image of infallibility and invincibility thus when their status is questioned, they tend to over-react even on the slightest things.

Many psychologists also identify people who are narcissistic, paranoid and sadistic as forms or character types of sociopaths. The thing is that there are different types of sociopaths and while many psychologists do not agree about the different character types of sociopaths, it is still important to take note that sociopaths are people who are devoid of feeling empathy towards other people.

17

Comorbidity of Sociopathy

It is often difficult to diagnose a person who is suffering from antisocial personality disorder. In most cases, they also co-morbidly exist with other diseases. This is the reason why the antisocial personality disorder is a complex condition. It is therefore important to know the types of conditions that also commonly exist with antisocial personality disorder. Below are the following conditions that also co-exist with antisocial personality disorder:

- Anxiety disorders
- Impulse control disorders
- Depressive disorders
- Attention deficit hyperactivity disorder
- Narcissistic personality disorder
- Sadistic personality disorder

It is also important to take note that when coupled with alcoholism and drugs, people who did not have any of the existing diseases that are comorbid with antisocial personality disorder may also show deficits on neurophyschological tests greater than those who are associated with the conditions mentioned above.

Effects of Antisocial Personality Disorder

The antisocial personality disorder affects not only the lives of people who are suffering from this condition but also the lives of people surrounding them. It threatens the physical well-being, social life as well as mental health of a person. So how does antisocial personality disorder affect a person? Read on.

Physical Effects

People who suffer from antisocial personality disorder can endanger their lives as well as the lives of other people. Below are the physical effects of this condition:

- Suicidal tendencies
- Insomnia or inability to sleep
- Physical assaults on oneself or to others
- Involvement in reckless or impulsive acts that can lead to injuries or even death
- Involvement in unsafe sexual behaviors

Psychological Effects

Perhaps the most evident effects of antisocial personality disorder are the psychological aspect of a person. Sufferers of this condition experience many psychological disturbances which, if left untreated, can cause the condition to worsen.

- Severe depression and likelihood of experiencing manic episodes
- Mood instability
- Emotional outbursts and the inability to regulate their emotions
- Panic attacks
- Suicidal ideations
- Aggressive or violent outbursts

Social Effects

AntIsocial personality disorder greatly impacts the social environmental setting of a person. People who suffer from antisocial behavior often experience the following:

- Inability to maintain or even start a relationship
- Damaged relationships due to destructive behaviors

- Isolation from other people due to their aggressive as well as manipulative behaviors
- Decreased performance in either school or work

Antisocial personality disorder has many bad effects to people and if these effects are not addressed nor treated by a professional, the person suffering from this condition will find it more difficult to connect with other people.

Chapter 2: Epidemiology, Prognosis and Treatment of Antisocial Personality Disorder

The antisocial personality disorder is often observed in 3% to 30% of all psychiatric admissions. The reason for this is that this personality disorder is comorbid to other types of personality disorders. Moreover, the prevalence of this disorder is also higher in specific populations including those who live in prisons where there is a high concentration of violent offenders. In fact, there are studies that indicate that 47% of male prisoners while 21% of female prisoners suffers from antisocial personality disorder. In a similar condition, people who entered in alcohol and drug addiction rehabilitation programs also have high tendencies to develop antisocial personality disorder.

On the other hand, it is also important to take note that this disorder is also not common in groups that are isolated from society in the survey conducted by the National Epidemiology Survey on Alcohol and Related Conditions, an estimated 30.8 million

American adults meet the diagnostic criteria for at least one personality disorder. In the recent survey, around 3.6% American adults are shown to suffer from antisocial personality disorder but it is alarming to take note that other personality disorders such as the paranoid personality disorder (4.4%), schizoid personality disorder (3.1%) and avoidant personality disorder (2.4%) are all comorbid or occurring with antisocial personality disorder.

It is also important to take note that the antisocial personality disorder is more likely to occur in males than females. However, the reason behind the gender specificity of the antisocial personality disorder is yet to be understood. On the other hand, below are very interesting statistics about the antisocial personality disorder.

- According to DSM-IV, the antisocial personality disorder in the US is spread between 1% adult females and 3% adult male.

- Research indicates that individuals who have antisocial personality disorder have exhibited behaviors of the disorder before the age of 15.
- Antisocial personality disorder is treatable but there are severe cases that cannot be reverted

thus 5.8% of the males while 1.2% of females have this condition for the rest of their lives.

- Prisons hold the highest number of psychopaths and sociopaths and about 80% of the male prison inmates show symptoms of antisocial personality disorder while 65% of imprisoned women have this condition.

- David Korten, professor from Harvard business school, noted that most high-ranking CEOs exhibit symptoms of antisocial personality disorder.

- Studies suggest that social environments play a very vital role in the development of antisocial personality disorder.

- People who suffer from this disorder are more likely to have experienced some form of abuse in childhood – physical, emotional or sexual.

Prognosis of Antisocial Personality Disorder

Not all people who suffer from antisocial personality disorder are withdrawn from society. In most cases, some are very charismatic. In fact, there are many business leaders as well as leaders of religious cults who showed symptoms of antisocial personality disorder and their conditions are not known until catastrophic results happen. For instance, multiple murders committed by Charles Manson and Reverend Jim Jones were famous individuals who were incarcerated for murder showed signs of antisocial personality disorder. Having said this, what is the prognosis of a person who is suffering from antisocial personality disorder?

According to Professor Emily Simonoff from the Institute of Psychiatry, antisocial personality disorder develops during the early childhood but is not detected until a person reaches adolescent. In most cases, childhood hyperactivity as well as conduct disorder is both linked to the early prediction of antisocial personality disorder and criminality. Moreover, having lower IQ levels and reading disabilities were very prominent indicators among children for preeminent antisocial personality disorder.

On the other hand, there are also several indicators that can tell whether a person is suffering from antisocial personality disorder. For instance, people who abuse drugs and alcohol and commit different crimes are likely to suffer from this disorder. People who suffer from mood problems and bipolar disorder also are vulnerable to this condition. Moreover, other types of personality disorders such as self-mutilation, narcissistic personality disorder and borderline personality disorder may also suffer from this condition.

Antisocial personality disorder makes the prognosis very difficult. Moreover, it also makes their treatment equally difficult. For instance, people who suffer from both sociopathy and schizophrenia are less likely to comply with treatment programs.

Treatment of Antisocial Personality Disorder

People who suffer from antisocial personality disorder should seek treatment. If not, the risks become magnified and this can cause danger not only to the person suffering from this condition but other people surrounding them as well. Treatment options among people who suffer from antisocial personality disorder can be challenging. In this section, the different treatment options will be discussed.

Types of Treatments Available For Antisocial Personality Disorder

- **Psychotherapy**: psychotherapy is the most common treatment to any personality disorder including those suffering from antisocial personality disorder. It is a process wherein the patients talk with their psychiatrists or psychologists. Psychotherapy is a great way for a sociopath to learn more how to be sensitive to the feelings of other people. Below are examples of psychotherapy methods used to treat antisocial personality disorder:

  - **Group or family psychotherapy** is one of the most common methods of psychotherapy which is a good option for young people who are suffering from antisocial personality disorder. This particular therapy method enlists the help of family members to reinforce the social support of the patient.

  - **Cognitive therapy** is a type of psychotherapy refers to the attempts of changing sociopathic ways of thinking.

- ○ Another type of therapy is the **behavior therapy** which uses rewards as well as punishment in order to promote good or bad behavior.

- ○ **Schema Therapy** is type of integrative psychotherapy that combines psychoanalytic, cognitive behavioral therapy and object relations theory. It is often used among people who fail to respond to the first treatment method thus patients who undergo this procedure are often considered as severe cases.

- **Medication:** Medication is often given to patients who are suffering from particular symptoms. It is important to take note, that there is no such thing as specific medication that can treat all people suffering from this condition. The common drugs that are used to treat the symptoms include serotonin reuptake inhibitors like sertraline and fluoxetine which reduces the irritability and aggressive behavior of a patient.

Unfortunately, antisocial personality disorder is one of the most complex personality disorders that afflict many individuals today. Many experts still argue about which treatment to use to help patients reduce their symptoms and revert their conditions back to normal.

Problems Encountered In Treating Patients with Antisocial Tendencies

Many behavioral experts noted that antisocial personality disorder is considered as the most difficult personality disorder to treat. Below are the problems encountered in treating people with antisocial personality disorders.

- **Late detection:** Generally, it is important for patients to seek help as early as possible as treatment is more likely to be successful if the patient has started earlier in life. Unfortunately, many people are not aware that they are suffering from this condition and often associate their aggression as normal mood swings.

- **No concept of remorse:** Another reason why people suffering from this condition are not successful in overcoming their condition is that they have little or no capacity for remorse and that they lack motivation to see the costs of their antisocial actions. Moreover, there are cases when patients who suffer from antisocial personality disorder stimulate remorse than commit to change thus they have the ability to be charming and manipulative for their own personal gains.

- **Lack of support from family members:** People who suffer from antisocial personality disorder need the support of their family members. Unfortunately, these are people who grow up in dysfunctional families thus it is difficult for them to get external support other than from their counselors and from their support groups.

- **No FDA-approved drugs to treat this disorder:** although psychiatrists give drugs like mood-stabilizing drugs, antidepressants and antipsychotic drugs to treat different symptoms like depression and aggression, there are any medications that are specific for treating antisocial personality disorder.

- **Therapist having negative feelings towards clients:** Due to the lack of concept of remorse, it is difficult for therapists to deal with clients suffering from antisocial personality disorder. The thing is that it is difficult to develop a sense of conscience among these people. Rather that, it is important for therapist to focus on rational arguments against repeating mistakes of their clients to build prosocial behavior.

Treating people who are suffering from antisocial personality behavior can be tough and while there is no one-size-fits-all cure, it is still crucial for patients to seek professional help to, at least, alleviate their symptoms or conditions so that they can function as normal and productive people in society.

Chapter 3: How to Deal with Sociopaths

Sociopaths are everywhere. As mentioned in the previous chapters, they come off as personable and even charming individuals but once they reveal their personalities, you will find out that they are not only manipulative but they are incapable of having remorse. Dealing with a sociopath can be emotionally draining and there is no sense in arguing with one. So how do you deal with a sociopath? Below are tips on how you can deal with sociopaths.

Understanding the Sociopath Behavior

Determining whether a person is a sociopath, or not, is the first step to understanding how to deal with one. Remember that sociopaths have a personality disorder that inhibits them from feeling empathy with other people. In Chapter 1, the signs and symptoms of antisocial personality disorder were given thus it is important that you create a checklist and see if a particular person whom you suspect of being one displays any of the signs indicated.

Another thing that you need to consider when determining a person's sociopathic behavior is his motivation. Remember that sociopaths are motivated to have power over other people. Thus, they are driven by the goal of achieving money, power, casual sex and other worldly things. You have to take note that if a sociopath appears to be good-hearted, there is always an ulterior motive for their kindness.

Since they lack remorse, sociopaths are expert manipulators thus it is important that you try to avoid being entangled with their schemes. In most cases, sociopaths like to pit other people against each other in order to achieve their end goals. Most sociopaths are involved in love triangles and are often the cause of marriage breakups. They also undermine their coworkers so that they can look good in front of their superiors.

Once you have identified that someone you know is a sociopath, it is important that you do not set any expectations that a particular sociopath will care about your feelings. Regardless whether you are a friend or not, a sociopath does not care who gets hurt or even used and they also take advantage to any signs of kindness that you show them. What you can do is to distance yourself enough so that you will realize that it is not about you. That way, you will have more power over a sociopath.

Lastly, in order to understand what sociopaths think, it is important that you also think like one. You have to remember that it is frustrating to deal with a person suffering from antisocial personality disorder just as you would a normal person. When you interact with a sociopath, always keep your guard up and show them that they have no power over you.

How to Communicate With a Sociopath

Communicating with a person suffering from antisocial personality disorder is different as you would communicate with a normal person. The thing is that it they aren't easy to deal with thus getting your message across can also be difficult. While it is easy to break off your relationship with a sociopathic friend, there are more cases wherein you cannot break things off with a sociopath as they might be your boss, sibling, child or even parent. For this reason, it is important that you learn effective ways on how to handle the situation. Below are the tips on how you can effectively communicate with a person suffering from antisocial personality disorder.

- **Put your guard up:** Sociopaths feed on empathy and use it against other people. When communicating with a sociopath, it is always important that you don't show your vulnerability with a sociopath. Showing your real emotions will make you an easy prey because a sociopath will think that you are a person who can easily be manipulated. When you interact with a sociopath, show him or her that you are in control of yourself. Try to put a cheerful face whenever a sociopath is around so you don't reveal your true mood. However, if you are feeling vulnerable, try to stay away from that person.

- **Be skeptical about whatever a sociopath tells you:** Remember that sociopaths are skilled at pushing people's buttons so make sure that you remain skeptical about what they tell you until you have done your own research.

- **Carry on with a neutral conversation:** To prevent being manipulated, it is important to speak during the conversation. This will also allow you to control the conversation so that it does not lead to anywhere unnecessary. Talk only about things that are neutral like weather, politics, sports and news. If you notice that he or she says something to harass you, change the topic if necessary. The main idea here is to not give a sociopath any room to feed on your vulnerabilities.

- **Do not share personal information:** The best way to be vulnerable to other people is to share information. Never talk to a sociopath about your friends, family, finances, dreams and other personal things. Remember that sociopaths will use you and everything that you hold dear so avoid talking about these things as well as those that will make you happy or upset.

How to Protect Yourself from a Sociopath

Protecting yourself from being manipulated by a sociopath is very important but with the ability of a sociopath to use anything against you, it is important that you work extra hard on how to avoid his or her advances. Below are tips on how you can protect yourself against sociopaths:

- **Don't reveal your cards:** If you plan on doing something, make sure that you have completed your tasks first before you share the information to other people. A sociopath who is determined to harass or humiliate you will find ways on knowing your plans and causing some troubles for you. If you work or live with a sociopath, make sure that you get things if they are not around.

- **Show a sociopath that you are on to him or her:** If you want a sociopath to be completely out of your life, make him or her realize that you will not give him or her power over you. If she harasses you, don't react and maintain a poker face in front of him or her. Calmly call that person out whenever they tell lies. By showing them that you are not someone who can easily be manipulated, they will stop harassing you and will move on to their next target.

- **Never become indebted to a sociopath:** One of the most important things that you should do is to not get yourself indebted to a sociopath. Sociopaths can use such situation to give them power over you. Decline any forms of help that a sociopath offers you and always have misgivings about the kindness that they show you because they might have underlying goals that they want to achieve from helping you.

- **Document the harassment:** Another way of protecting yourself from sociopaths is to collect evidence so that you will have proof that you were being wronged by a sociopath. Save email transcripts or exchanges using your mobile phone so that you can share it to parties involved. Nothing irks a sociopath more than being caught in the middle of his or her lies. However, when recording evidences, make sure that you don't commit an act of felony. You might want to seek legal counsel first if you want to proceed.

- **Seek professional help:** Ironically, it is not only sociopaths that need to seek help but also their victims. If you feel emotionally drained, then talk with someone who can help you.

Professionals can give you more tips on how to protect yourself with a sociopath.

Conclusion

People who suffer from antisocial personality disorder are those who are incapable of empathy and remorse and it is extremely difficult to deal with them. Although there are treatments that are available, most sociopaths don't seek treatment because they believe that there is nothing wrong with them. Unfortunately, there are no effective treatments methods that are available to date that can help people suffer from this condition. What is needed is for immediate people who deal with sociopaths to know how to handle people with such condition.